DACHSHUNDS
COLORING BOOK

Welcome to our Dachshund Coloring Book!

Prepare for a charming journey of creativity and relaxation with our lovable 'wiener dogs'. Each page presents a delightful dachshund design waiting for your personal touch of color. Regardless of your skill level, you'll find joy in bringing these adorable creatures to life.

Sprinkled throughout the book are fun facts about dachshunds, adding an educational twist to your artistic adventure. Remember, there are no rules in coloring - it's your creative journey. Enjoy the tranquility it brings and celebrate the captivating charm of dachshunds.

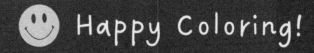 Happy Coloring!

THIS
COLORING BOOK
BELONGS TO

....

Dachshunds are often described as 'half a dog high and a dog and a half long,' capturing their unique proportions perfectly.

TEST COLOR PAGE

Despite their size, Dachshunds are known to have a large personality packed into a small body.

A Dachshund was the first Olympic mascot — his name was Waldi, and he represented the 1972 Olympics in Munich, Germany.

Queen Victoria was a fan of the breed and had several pet Dachshunds.

Dachshunds are excellent watchdogs with a big bark for their size.

Dachshunds are actually excellent diggers, thanks to their strong and short legs.

Dachshunds have a unique running style, moving in a sequence of diagonal pairs, which gives them speed and stamina despite their small stature.

Dachshunds are known to have an excellent memory. They remember friends (and foes) even after long periods of time.

The long-haired variety of Dachshunds were supposedly bred with St. Bernards, which gave them their unique, silky coats.

Dachshunds are known to have a playful and mischievous nature. They're always up for fun and games!

Their long noses enhance a Dachshund's sense of smell, and their deep chests provide lung capacity for stamina when hunting.

Dachshunds can have different types of ears – the shorthaired variety has ears that are medium in length, while the longhaired ones have slightly longer ears.

Dachshunds love to burrow, and it's not uncommon to find them snuggled under a blanket.

Dachshunds are surprisingly good climbers, often surprising their owners with their agility.

The Dachshund is the only AKC-recognized breed that hunts both above and below ground.

Dachshunds are often associated with Germany, but the first breed club was founded in England in 1881.

Their iconic body shape is due to a gene mutation. This trait has been purposely bred into them because it allows them to get into small spaces during hunting.

Despite their small size,
Dachshunds need regular exercise
and mental stimulation.
They love playing with toys
and solving puzzles!

Dachshunds are great travel buddies — they're small and adaptable, making them great companions for your adventures.

Dachshunds can be very vocal and often 'talk' to their owners with unique sounds and barks.

Their expressive faces and big, soulful eyes are part of the reason Dachshunds are so beloved around the world.

Despite being small,
Dachshunds are courageous.
They were originally bred
to hunt badgers,
which are known to be
quite fierce.

Dachshunds live fairly long lives for dogs, often living to be over 12-15 years old. Their longevity is just one more reason to love them!

Dachshunds are nicknamed 'wiener dogs' due to their long, hot dog-like shape, but they actually existed before hot dogs. The hot dog sausages were called 'dachshund sausages' before they were named hot dogs!

Dachshunds have a great sense of smell! Only second to Bloodhounds, they have about 125 million scent receptors.

Thank you for spending your time with us and our whimsical dachshunds!

It's been a pleasure taking you on this colorful journey, and we hope you enjoyed every moment as much as we enjoyed creating it. Your support and enthusiasm are the very heart of our work.

To help us continue making fun and imaginative coloring books, we kindly ask for your feedback. If you could spare a moment to leave an honest review on Amazon, we would greatly appreciate it. Your insights not only help us improve, but also allow fellow coloring enthusiasts to discover our books.

Once again, thank you so much for joining us on this coloring adventure. We hope to see you again in our future books. Until then, keep those colors flowing and always remember: the world is your canvas!

Made in the USA
Las Vegas, NV
23 November 2024